Beyond Lean

Lessons for Leading Organizational Change

Darrell Bender

Heuristic Books

Chesterfield, Missouri USA

Copyright Notice:

ISBN 1-59630-016-7

Library of Congress Cataloging in Publication
        Library of Congress Cataloging-in-Publication Data

Bender, Darrell, 1965-
  Beyond lean : lessons for leading organizational change / Darrell Bender.
     p. cm.
  ISBN 1-59630-016-7 (alk. paper)
  1. Organizational change. 2. Leadership. I. Title.
  HD58.8.B4586 2006
  958.4'092--dc22

                              2006022131

Heuristic Books is an imprint of

Heuristic Books
for Mathematics & Management Science
heuristicbooks.com

Science & Humanities Press
PO Box 63006
Chesterfield MO 63006-7151
636-394-4950
Heuristicbooks.com

From The Author

Today's business leaders must seek new and creative means to offset the entourage of ominous external threats their businesses face daily.

Due to its numerous foretold business improvement success stories, *Lean Manufacturing* captures the interest of many aspiring leaders. However, for a multitude of reasons, not all business leaders that attempt *Lean* transformations attain their desired goal.

Uncovering the importance of Leadership during organizational change efforts, the story that follows portrays a fictional organization, setting and characters, and the challenges they faced during an attempted *Lean Enterprise* transformation.

I hope that you find the story insightful and inspiring!

Darrell Bender,

March 2006

Dedication

I dedicate this book to my wife Kim, and my dear friend Leon. Without them, and their support, this book would not have been possible.

I would also like to express my sincere thanks to all of the men and women that I have had the distinct pleasure of working with over the past 20 years. Some, I have chosen to emulate, and others have taught me how not to behave. Good or bad, I have learned from all of them, and for that, I am eternally grateful!

About the Author

Compassionate and caring by nature, yet driven to succeed and tempted by the intoxicating wealth and power that lay atop the corporate ladder, Darrell Bender frequently found himself facing internal struggles in his role as the Lean Manufacturing and Continuous Improvement Manager for a hundred million dollar corporation.

Feeling enlightened and compelled to walk a different path in life; Darrell departed from his quest to climb the corporate ladder, and embarked upon a journey as a Lean Manufacturing business consultant.

Throughout his corporate and consulting experiences, at only 41 years of age, Darrell has personally led and witnessed many organizational change initiatives. His experiences have led him to believe that Leadership is the deciding factor that ultimately determines success or failure.

Through his published literary works, Darrell hopes to teach others to see that organizational change is at its best when skillful leaders exhibit humanitarian values, rather than greed and power.

Table of Contents

Windy Point

This story begins early one summer morning in the aging little town of Windy Point.

The sun had not yet risen above the eastern skyline, when Leon and his grandfather finished loading their fishing gear into the back of Grandpa's pick-up truck.

Leon's grandfather, a retired history teacher with almost 80 years of life experience, has gray hair and bushy mustache. His eyes are adorned with round, wire rimmed glasses, and from a distance, he bares a slight resemblance to Albert Einstein. Although his body is plagued by arthritis, Leon's Grandfather enjoys the outdoors, and his two favorite hobbies are fishing and gardening.

Leon is a short but physically fit young man. His hair is brown and he has kept the crew-cut style he received in the military some years earlier. Although he possesses a terrific sense of humor, Leon rarely shows it at work. His peers gave him the nickname "Sgt. Carter" because of his businesslike work ethic, military experience, and physical resemblance to the character portrayed in the television show.

Leon is the Continuous Improvement Manager at Hardwood Floor Systems (HFS), and has had that role for a little more than three years. Prior to that, Leon was a cracker-jack production supervisor at HFS for about six years.

HFS is a manufacturer of all types of residential and industrial grade hardwood flooring. Because their vast product breadth and offerings equate to nearly two million different products, they are a make-to-order manufacturer.

At its high, HFS employed nearly 1000 employees. Today that number has shrunk to around 600, 450 of whom are hourly employees and the remaining are salaried. Because it employs so many people, HFS is vital to Windy Point's economic stability.

HFS has had several different owners and business names over the past century.

An entrepreneur named John Rodman originally founded it in the early 1900's.

Being an entrepreneur, John Rodman recognized at an early age there was a growing need for lumber and wood products, to support the commercial and residential building boom that was taking place in Windy Point and other outlying communities.

John saved his money to purchase the tools and equipment he needed to set up a small sawmill behind his father's machine shed. He began sawing rough framing lumber at first, but many of his customers asked if he could provide finished lumber for cabinets, flooring and trim.

Inspired by his customer's demand, John took a risk and borrowed the money he needed to move his business into Windy Point, purchased additional equipment, and hired a couple of young men to help him fill his ever-growing customer's orders.

As his small business grew into a 100 million dollar corporation over the next half century, John knew that his success would not have been possible without his customers, suppliers, and employees. His actions were guided by his father's motto that was burned into his memory at a young age, much as a brand is burned into a calf.

Hard work, perseverance, and do onto others as you would like done onto yourself.

John's father told him that if he did those three things, his life would be filled with a richness that went far beyond mere money.

John knew all of his employees on a first name basis, and frequently spoke with them during his regular walks through the plant. Employees looked forward to John's frequent visits and sincere praises. They knew he took a real interest in them by the way he asked about their families, friends, and hobbies.

John gave back to the community in which his business was located by funding the building of the first city park and contributing heavily to school building projects.

Residents of Windy Point jumped at the chance to become employees at Rodman's Saw Mill, largely due to John Rodman's reputation of being an honest, hardworking and compassionate businessperson.

John worked long hours and never married. Many said that he was married to his work. When John's health began to fail him in the 1960's, he sold his business to the Eastwood Corporation.

Eastwood Corporation was a multi-billion dollar enterprise with many diverse business holdings, headquartered near Boston.

After the business changed hands, Eastwood executives changed the name from Rodman's Sawmill to Eastwood Lumber Products, and replaced the incumbent executive leadership team with their own business managers. Fear of additional staff changes rippled through the remaining mid and lower level managers.

After two years of declining sales, primarily caused by non-competitive pricing of several products, Eastwood Lumber Product's executive management group decided to narrow the product offerings and restructure the labor pool. They focused on becoming the market leader of residential and industrial hardwood flooring products. The business name was changed to Eastwood Floor Systems as part of their marketing strategy. Production of non-flooring products stopped, and 75 hourly and eight salaried employees were laid off. This was the first significant downsizing that the hourly employees had experienced and it sent a shockwave of fear throughout the plant. Unfortunately, the top-level business leaders did nothing to address these fears, and rumors of additional lay-offs fanned the flames of fear and anxiety.

Employees didn't care much for the new atmosphere that quickly evolved in the plant since the new management team had taken over. Managers spent a great deal of time in their offices crunching numbers or in business meetings planning cost reductions. Workers only saw or heard from the business managers if there was criticism to be handed out, or when a new cost reduction initiative was being launched. Employees began to feel that they were not valued. Most of them missed the personal interaction that John Rodman had always made time for in years past.

Labor and management relations steadily deteriorated. Layoffs and the lack of positive interaction between management and employees fostered mistrust and fear, and eventually prompted the hourly employees to organize and join a labor union.

After the employees organized, labor and management relations deteriorated even faster. There was a definite "we" versus "them" mentality within both parties. Customers bore the brunt of internal conflict that raged within the plant in the form of late shipments, higher pricing, and quality related issues. Eastman's monthly profit and loss statement revealed the negative impact of declining sales.

Corporate officers reacted by changing the local business leadership team frequently over the next couple of decades.

Each new management team brought their unique set of values and skill sets. They each tried different "canned programs" to improve business profits. Total Quality Circles, Employee Involvement Groups, and High Performance Work Teams just to name a few. Although the improvement processes were different, the attempted implementation was typically the same. Top management would attempt to market and sell their wares to the union. When their efforts were met with opposition, they would hand off their implementation responsibilities to the mid and lower level managers, who would push until near exhaustion. Eventually the management team would give up their cause, blaming the Union for their failed efforts. This repeated start and stop mentality unintentionally threw Eastwood Floor Systems into the ever-popular *"Flavor of the Month Club"*.

Consequently, both salaried and hourly employees developed a skeptical *THIS TOO SHALL PASS* attitude. Although managers did not intend to reward employees for resisting change, managers giving up after a period of resistance did just that. As a result, the workforce grew increasingly resistant to change and became quite undisciplined as the years progressed. Although managers could not see it at the time, the lack of workforce discipline would turn out to be a significant obstacle in the years ahead.

Even though the multi-million dollar business was still turning a marginal profit annually, Eastwood's corporate officers grew tired of dealing with the ongoing personnel issues at the Windy Point plant, so they decided to sell the business. It goes without saying that Eastwood did not air their dirty laundry to prospective buyers. Prospects were told that Eastwood was going through a business restructuring and that Eastwood Floor Systems did not meet their core business criteria.

A small group of unsuspecting private investors purchased Eastwood Floor Systems in the late 1980's, and they renamed the business Hardwood Floor Systems (HFS).

Because the new owners lacked manu-facturing experience, they hired Mr. Ritz as Chief Executive Officer to manage their newest acquisition. Mr. Ritz is a well-educated, wealthy man, with over twenty years of business experience to his credit. His background was primarily in marketing, and this would be his first experience as a CEO.

Mr. Ritz was a hands-off leader, who preferred to wine and dine customers rather than pay close attention to the numerous details needed to manage a business. He typically deferred the detail responsibility to others.

Mr. Ritz hired Mr. Gump as Chief Operating Officer (C.O.O.) to assist with the business improvement and growth he desired.

Mr. Gump had 25 years of experience in the wood cabinet manufacturing industry. Most recently, he was the General Manager of a small custom cabinet plant located in the upper mid-west.

Although he is not as wealthy as Mr. Ritz was, Mr. Gump was very much into material possessions. He only drove expensive vehicles and wore designer clothes. When he moved to the Windy Point area, he purchased two contiguous building lots on the shores of Stainy Lake, and promptly had a 5,000 sq ft home built for him and his wife.

Mr. Gump was a braggart, and had a tendency to exaggerate the truth to suit his needs. He flaunted his possessions, and was always boasting about his successes from frequent chartered hunting or fishing trips.

Gump was a very poor listener and seldom valued what others had to say. The only good ideas were usually his own, and if things turned out poorly, Gump was quick to lay the blame on someone else. He earned the nickname "Mr. Teflon" because everyone knew that nothing bad *stuck* to him.

The work culture at HFS changed under Gump's leadership, and it was not for the better. The plant rapidly became dirty and dark. Equipment preventative maintenance was non-existent, and most machines were riddled with fluid leaks and breakdowns. Quality controls were no longer used and defects routinely reached the customers. Shipments were later than ever, absentee-ism was on the rise, injuries were commonplace, morale was on the decline, and customer satisfaction reached a new low.

The Voyage Begins

Leon and his grandfather arrived at the Stainy Lake public boat launch just as dawn was breaking. As they exited the truck, they could feel a cool northwesterly breeze on their faces. The familiar smell of algae bloom and fishy water unique to Stainy Lake quickly filled their nostrils. Both Leon and his grandfather knew that the breeze, if it lasted, would help beat the mid-day heat and blow away most of the biting insects that frequently satisfied their hunger by feeding on unsuspecting anglers.

Leon and Grandpa carefully slid the old wooden rowboat from the back of the pick-up truck, and lashed it to the boat dock. This was a slow process, since Grandpa's arthritis prevented him from moving very quickly. After they loaded their gear and lunch into the boat, Leon parked the truck. When Leon returned to the boat dock, he found that Grandpa had already climbed into the boat and assumed the oarsman position. Leon asked, "Are you sure you don't want me to row, Grandpa?"

"The rowing does my arthritis good, and it helps to keep me limber. Climb in and let's get going," Grandpa responded.

Knowing that it would be futile to argue with his grandpa, Leon pushed the boat away from the dock as he leapt into it. Leon and his grandpa were both looking forward to a day filled with good company, fun, and much deserved relaxation. What they didn't know, was that the trip would prove to be life changing!

There wasn't an abundance of natural structure in Stainy Lake, so Leon and his grandfather decided to begin fishing around the docks that the local residents had put in. The docks seemed to attract and hold baitfish, which drew in the game fish they were after.

As they drifted near the first dock, Grandpa said, "I'll bet you a root beer that I'll catch the first fish."

"You're on!" Leon replied.

While they fished, Leon and his grandpa reminisced about past fishing trips. Leon

14

loved to listen to his grandpa tell fishing stories from years past.

Only 15 minutes had passed when Leon's grandpa started shouting. "Get the net, I've got one on!"

Leon dropped his fishing rod and grabbed the net. Before Leon could even get to him, Grandpa had already brought the fish into the boat. After a quick measurement Grandpa proclaimed, "Close, but no cigar, it needs another inch to be legal. None the less, a bet is a bet and you still owe me a root beer!" Grandpa said with a grin, as he released the fish back into the lake with a small splash. "Hand me another night crawler," he asked, holding out his hand.

Leon reached into the worm box and pulled out a plump night crawler. The worm wriggled and squirmed in an attempt to break free from Leon's tight grip, but it was to no avail. As Leon handed the night crawler to Grandpa, he asked, "What do you say we go double or nothing for the biggest fish of the day?"

"Oh, you must be feeling lucky. You're on!" Grandpa replied with a sense of confidence.

The action proved to be slow for the next several hours, and as the morning passed, Leon and his grandfather ran out of small talk and stories to tell one another. Their minds began to wander as the silence settled in.

Looking across the Lake at Gump's mansion, Leon was reminded of the problems he was having at work. He began to wonder if his grandfather would be able to help him sort out the mess, he had gotten into.

Leon began to speak with a serious but apprehensive tone, "Grandpa… I have a problem at work."

"What is it?" Grandpa asked.

"I'm thinking about quitting my job," Leon responded.

Taken back by Leon's comment, his grandfather asked, "It must be serious, if you're thinking about quitting. I have never known you to quit at anything. Have you spoken to your father about this?"

"No. I don't think dad would understand. You know how he is. He would probably just tell me to be a man and suck it up," Leon replied.

"Well, your father can lack patience at times. Why don't you tell me what's on your mind?" Grandpa said.

Leon began to explain the situation to his grandfather. "It all started about four years ago when Eastwood sold the business. I was a supervisor at the time, and things were not going well from a financial perspective. Mr. Ritz, the Chief Executive Officer down at the plant, was receiving pressure from the owners to increase the market share, and grow the profits. Mr. Ritz met with Mr. Gump, the Chief Operating Officer, and told him that the investors were not pleased with the financial performance of the business, and that he had better get things turned around quickly, or he would find someone that could."

"Sounds like Mr. Ritz tightened the thumb screws on Mr. Gump. How did Gump plan to get things turned around? Grandpa asked.

"Gump remembered a couple of articles that he recently read about *Lean Manufacturing*, and the almost miraculous impact it had on organizations. Gump thought, if *Lean Manufacturing* could improve others' performance, it would surely be the silver bullet that would fix all of his problems."

"Mr. Gump told Mr. Ritz that *Lean Manufacturing* would fix all of their problems, increase profits and get the investors off their backs. Gump's enthusiasm was convincing. Mr. Ritz told Mr. Gump to forge ahead with his improvement plans."

"Wait a minute Leon. Didn't you say that Gump had only *read* about *Lean Manufacturing*? Did he have any practical application experience?" Grandpa asked.

"That's right. He had only read about other's success stories. Gump didn't have any practical application experience," Leon replied.

"Didn't Mr. Ritz ask how *Lean Manufacturing* was going to fix their problems?" Grandpa asked.

"No. Mr. Ritz doesn't have a strong manufacturing background and he is not detail oriented. He prefers to schmooze with customers," Leon replied.

Grandpa paused briefly and said, "I see. Forgive me for asking Leon, but what is *Lean Manufacturing?*"

Leon explained, "Simply put, *Lean Manufacturing,* or *Lean Enterprise* as it is sometimes referred, is a systematic process that helps people to recognize and eliminate waste throughout all aspects of their business."

"Sounds simple, but I'm sure it's more involved than that," Grandpa replied.

"You can say that again. Because Mr. Gump did not fully understand *Lean Manufacturing,* he had no idea what he was getting us into when he told Mr. Ritz that *Lean* was the solution to all of our problems," Leon responded.

Threats Abound

Leon went on to explain to his grandpa how Mr. Gump hired a business consultant named Mr. Cuttmore to assist with the *Lean Enterprise* transformation.

"Mr. Cuttmore met with Mr. Gump, the manufacturing managers and all of the supervisors. We reviewed a 180-slide PowerPoint presentation that provided an overview of *Lean Manufacturing.*

Grandpa interjected, "Hold on a minute. You reviewed a 180-slide presentation in one day?"

"More like four hours," Leon replied.

"Don't take this wrong Leon, but how did Cuttmore expect you to retain all of that information in such a short period of time?" Grandpa asked.

"He didn't. It was more of a sales pitch and overview than actual training. Cutt-more's presentation was compelling, and his knowledge of manufacturing and

21

economics was very impressive. I remember wishing that all of the Executive and Union Leaders would have been present to hear what he had to say."

"What were some of the things he told you?" Grandpa asked.

Leon outlined how Mr. Cuttmore explained that businesses face numerous external threats. "He told us that Federal, State, and Local Government officials affect the business world by the decisions they make."

Leon must have touched a hot button, because Grandpa shouted and scoffed, "That's an understatement! Free Trade, what were they thinking? It seems that you can't pick up the paper or turn on the evening news anymore without learning of more lost manufacturing jobs. How are we supposed to compete with other countries' low labor rates?"

Leon, trying to calm his grandpa down, replied, "We spoke with Mr. Cuttmore about that very issue for some time. He explained how free trade agreements, the Internet, and ever-improving worldwide rapid transit system have created a *Global* marketplace."

"Mr. Cuttmore told us that *Global* competition frequently creates a *buyer's* market due to lower pricing and excess manufacturing capacity. He said sales managers typically respond to this by slashing their prices in an effort to keep their market share. This reaction typically reduces business profitability, and businesses are forced to begin rapid and extreme cost cutting measures."

"Mr. Cuttmore told us that he has seen this pattern many times, and it usually has a less than desirable ending for all parties involved. He cautioned us not to get caught up in price wars, and encouraged us to develop close, lasting relationships with our customers and to learn what they value, and to use that information to gain a competitive advantage."

"Did he explain how to go about doing that?" Grandpa asked.

"I don't recall all of the details, but essentially he would help us to develop a brief questionnaire that would be used to interview a cross-section of our customers to determine what motivated their purchase decisions. He stressed the importance of recording their responses verbatim."

"Why was that so important?" Grandpa asked.

"Mr. Cuttmore told us that if we wrote their responses in our own words, we would be influencing the data and the outcome would be compromised," Leon replied.

Grandpa added, "Makes sense. Please, go on."

"We would evaluate our customer's responses and look for common themes. Once we had them identified and documented, we would use the information to create a correlation table of features and benefits. We would then use the information derived from the table to write a *Value Proposition* statement that would guide us in our business planning and decision making processes."

Grandpa interrupted Leon, "Clever! The *Value Proposition* would align your decisions with your customer's needs. But how would you ensure delivery of those needs?"

24

"We were going to use *Lean Manufacturing* principles and tools to ensure delivery of the *Value Proposition* to our customers. Mr. Cuttmore told us that our *Value Proposition* combined with *Lean Manufacturing* principles would help us create a unique selling position that would help to thwart competitive threats," Leon responded.

"I'm no businessman, but Mr. Cuttmore's recommendations make sense to me. What did HFS's customers say they valued?" Grandpa asked.

Leon gave a heavy sigh, and painfully replied to his grandpa's question. "We never had a chance to find out. After Mr. Cuttmore left, Gump told us that we did not have the time or money to go interview a bunch of customers. He said that consultants were experts at wasting other's money, and that we had been in the hardwood flooring business a long time, and that if our sales staff didn't know what our customers needed by now, they should all be fired!"

"What did you think about Gump's reaction to Cuttmore's suggestion?" Grandpa asked.

"I was very disappointed with his decision. With all the competitive threats that HFS faces every day, (both foreign and domestic) I believe that we need to be ever vigilant, and constantly seeking a competitive advantage," Leon replied.

"Did you express your concerns to Mr. Gump?" Grandpa asked.

"I was going to, but am I ever glad I didn't," Leon responded.

"Why's that?" Grandpa asked with a quizzical look.

"One of the managers who were present beat me to it, and if looks could kill, I would have witnessed a murder. Gump's face turned fire engine red and the veins popped out on his forehead as he glared at the manager. Gump couldn't contain his anger and he berated the manager in front of everyone," Leon replied.

Grandpa, having difficulty believing what he had just heard, said, "A man of Gump's position should know better than to behave in that manner."

26

Leon responded, "Yeah. I sure felt bad for the manager, but we all learned a valuable lesson that day."

"What's that?" Grandpa asked.

"To keep our ears open and mouths shut!" Leon exclaimed.

Grandpa did not respond to Leon's comment, but he could not help but think that external threats were the least of HFS's problems.

Just then, Leon felt the end of his fishing rod spring sharply towards the water's surface. He instinctively reefed back on the rod to set the hook! The drag screamed, as fishing line ripped off the spool.

As he had done many times in the past, Leon's grandpa instinctively shouted commands, "Don't horse him! Loosen your drag or he'll break your line! Take it easy now. Keep him away from the dock or he'll wrap the line on you!"

Leon played the fish perfectly, loosening the drag when needed, and applying pressure at just the right times. Before long, the fish tired, and Leon brought it to the surface along side the boat. Leon and

Grandpa peered at the fish, their eyes bulging with satisfaction.

Grandpa yelled, "It's a big walleye, pushing 25 inches in length and close to 7 pounds I'd say! Bring it around this way. Careful now, you don't want to lose it!"

Leon's heart pounded in his chest and his hands trembled with excitement. This was the biggest fish he had ever fought.

Grandpa forgot about his age and painful arthritis, and with the speed and agility of a 20 year old, he plunged the net into the water and scooped up the walleye.

"We'll be eating fresh fish tonight!" Grandpa shouted, as he licked his lips in anticipation.

Grandpa shook Leon's hand, patted him on the shoulder and congratulated him on how well he had played the fish.

Leon hoisted the walleye from the net, and carefully removed the jig from its toothy mouth.

Pulling out a disposable camera from his inside shirt pocket, Grandpa said, "Hold it up so I can capture the moment forever."

Grandpa didn't need to remind Leon to smile. After Grandpa was satisfied that he had taken a good photo, Leon hooked the walleye onto a stringer that was attached to the boat. Leon stared at the fish for a few moments as he eased the fish into the water, and although he was very excited, he felt a sense of sorrow knowing that the fish had made the ultimate sacrifice for his benefit.

It was difficult for Leon to re-tip his jig with a fresh night crawler, because his hands still trembled from excitement. After several tries, Leon managed to thread the crawler onto the hook. As Leon cast his bait back into the water, he said, "Remember, you agreed, double or nothing for the biggest fish of the day."

"Don't count your chickens before they hatch Leon. The day isn't over yet," Grandpa replied with confidence.

Waste Ho!

For 15 minutes or so, Leon had forgotten all about his work troubles, as he had been consumed with the joy of sharing the experience of catching a big fish with his grandfather.

After the replaying and retelling of the fish story had ended, and after Leon and his grandpa had thoroughly fished the spot in search of another walleye, Grandpa asked Leon to go on with his story.

"After our initial meeting with Mr. Cuttmore, the area manufacturing managers met with him privately and they drew out the current flow of raw materials, products, and information throughout their areas of the factory. They called the drawings *Current State Value Stream Maps*," Leon told his Grandpa.

"How did Mr. Cuttmore come up with the name *Value Stream* maps?" Grandpa asked.

"I'm not sure of the origin. But if I had to guess I would say it's because the maps contain information that allows us to see the difference between wasteful and value adding activities," Leon replied.

"Seems reasonable, please, go on," Grandpa said.

"The maps revealed that more than 97 percent of HFS's manufacturing lead-time was non value-adding!" Leon exclaimed.

Leon's Grandfather looked at Leon in disbelief and asked, "You mean to tell me that the employees at HFS are standing around doing nothing for 97 percent of their workday? No wonder Mr. Ritz is coming down on Gump. He should have been fired a long time ago for letting that go on."

Before his grandpa could say another word, Leon replied, "No, no. Employees are not standing around for 97 percent of their workday. The percentage isn't a reflection of individual employees' performance; it represents the process as a whole."

Grandpa, appearing puzzled said, "I'm not sure I'm following you, Leon."

Leon, remembering that his grandfather lacked a manufacturing background, realized that he needed to use an analogy to which his grandpa would relate.

Leon thought for a moment and then began to speak, "Let me try to explain it another way. You use a riding lawnmower to mow your lawn, right?"

"Yes" his Grandpa replied.

"How wide is the cutting path?" Leon asked.

"36 inches, it has two 18 inch blades," His Grandpa replied.

"How long does it take you to mow your lawn?" Leon asked.

"I've got it down to about an hour," Grandpa replied, with a look of accomplishment.

"Are your lawnmower's blades always engaged, and are you utilizing their full cutting width the entire time you operate your lawn mower?" Leon asked.

Grandpa lowered his eyebrows, thought for a moment, and then replied, "No. I overlap my cutting path by at least a couple of inches so I don't miss any spots, and there are times when I disengage the blades while I'm driving across the sidewalk and driveway, and I need to back up occasionally when I am maneuvering around obstacles."

"What percentage of the time would you estimate that you spend cutting grass, versus operating your lawn mower?" Leon asked.

"I would say that 90 percent of the time is spent cutting the grass," Grandpa responded.

"You're not standing around on break for the remaining 10 percent, are you?" Leon asked.

"Heck no!" Grandpa exclaimed.

Leon, sensing that his grandfather was becoming upset, reassured him by responding, "I didn't think so. You see, the *process* of mowing your lawn has some inherent waste built into it. To eliminate missed spots, you overlap the blades along each adjacent path. Since you are not utilizing the full width of your blades on each pass, you are required to make more passes, which extends your mowing time. Your yard is rectangular, and it has a driveway, sidewalks, trees, buildings, and other obstacles that interfere with your ability to cut 100 percent of the time. You see, the design and process creates waste."

"Doesn't the operator play a part in the process?" Grandpa asked.

"Absolutely! The operator has the ability to increase or reduce waste by the way he operates the mower."

"Thanks. That clears things up," Grandpa said.

Leon, sensing that his grandpa had not fully appreciated the magnitude of the problem that HFS faced with so much waste, asked, "What would you say if I asked you to change the way you mow your lawn? What if I asked you to mow for 3 seconds, then stop and idle for 97 seconds, and to keep repeating this process until you were done mowing? Or, what if I asked you to replace the mower's two 18 inch blades with a single 1 inch blade and mow the lawn non stop until you were done?" Leon asked his grandfather.

"I would say that you must think I have gone soft in the head, if you expect me to accept either of those suggestions," his grandpa replied with a half-serious chuckle.

Leon exclaimed, "Of course you would. Anyone with half a brain would think that I was crazy for suggesting such ludicrous ideas. Yet that's exactly what the *Current State Value Stream Maps* revealed was going on at HFS; and it was accepted by employees as the way we do business!"

"Wow! I'm not a businessman, but I would say HFS better get things turned around in a hurry, or it won't be around much longer," Grandpa urged Leon.

Leon replied, "Mr. Cuttmore reassured us that we were comparable to most U.S. manufacturers. He said that it is not uncommon for U.S. manufacturers to have 95 percent or more of their manufacturing lead-time consumed by wasteful activities. He explained that wasteful activities included things like:

- Defects, rework and/or scrap

- <u>O</u>verproduction of parts that aren't needed by downstream processes

- <u>W</u>aiting for materials, information, equipment, or people

- <u>N</u>on value-added processing, unnecessary handling, or over engineering a product that customers aren't willing to pay for

- <u>T</u>ransportation of parts throughout the process

- <u>I</u>nventories that are not necessary

- <u>E</u>xcess people motion, reaching, squatting, walking, bending, etc."

"I noticed that the seven wasteful activities you listed create the acronym: DOWNTIE. If there was an "M" between the "I" and "E", it would spell DOWNTIME," Grandpa stated.

"Good observation! The "M" could stand for the lost money associated with unplanned downtime," Leon replied.

"Okay, so the maps revealed the waste, what was your plan to get rid of it?" Grandpa asked.

All Hands on Deck

"Good question Grandpa. Let me explain what happened next," Leon responded.

"After the *Current State Value Stream Maps* were completed, Gump met with the area managers and the supervisors to discuss next steps. Gump told us that Mr. Cuttmore's presentation indicated that we needed to begin using empowered cross-functional teams to effect rapid improvements within our business to eliminate waste. Gump said that Cuttmore's presentation referred to the rapid improvement process as a *Blitz*."

"One of the area managers asked Gump if Mr. Cuttmore was going to facilitate our *Blitzes*. Gump turned bright red in the face and began to lecture everyone present, saying, 'That's what you people are paid to do. If there is anyone here that is not comfortable in leading a cross-functional problem solving team, there is the door!

Would anyone like to leave? If so, now is the time.'"

"Did anyone leave?" Grandpa asked.

"No. However, the thought probably ran through everyone's mind. Not because they were afraid of facilitating *Blitzes*, but due to Gump's unprofessional demeanor," Leon responded.

Grandpa, feeling bad for the tyranny that Leon was subjected to, and shaking his fist, proclaimed, "Boy, it's a good thing I wasn't there. I would have told Gump where to get off!"

"I think everyone would have paid to see that Grandpa," Leon said with a chuckle.

"I didn't mean to interrupt your story Leon, please go on," Grandpa urged.

"After his lecture, Gump assigned *Blitz* quotas to each area manager and stormed out of the room. Keep in mind that the area managers were not trained in *Blitz* facilitation, and some quickly passed the responsibility onto their respective supervisors, who were not trained either."

"Sounds like a game of hot potato," Grandpa scoffed.

"It was. But right, wrong, or indifferent, Gump had communicated his expectations, so we began to *Blitz*," Leon replied.

"How did the organization react to the *Blitzes*?" Grandpa asked.

Leon replied, "Employees that weren't on the Blitz team were mostly confused."

"Why's that?" Grandpa asked.

"Most likely because there was no formal announcement to the organization explaining the Blitz process or what areas were going to be impacted," Leon replied.

"You have got to be kidding. Isn't that like going into battle and not sharing your battle plans with your allies? Isn't there a high risk of friendly fire incidents?" Grandpa asked.

"I wish I were kidding. To answer your question, it was like going into battle without communicating with our allies, and yes, we did suffer friendly fire casualties, figuratively speaking," Leon replied.

"How did participants react to the *Blitzes*?" Grandpa asked.

"Most members were at least neutral when the *Blitz*es first began, but they gradually became opposed to the process when so-called *empowered Blitz* teams were not allowed to implement the changes they recommended," Leon replied.

"Why weren't teams allowed to implement their recommended changes?" Grandpa queried.

"I suppose it was due to a number of reasons, but it really boils down to poor leadership," Leon replied.

"How so?" Grandpa asked.

"Project team leaders were responsible for the upfront planning which included things like:

- Defining the project scope
- Establishing measurable objectives
- Coordinating resources
- Identifying team boundary conditions
- Member selection

Unfortunately, most of the managers and supervisors were never trained in project management and were unaware of the importance of the upfront planning. As a result, project teams were often faced with project "scope creep", poorly defined or immeasurable objectives, resource constraints, and surprise boundary conditions that surfaced after the team had reached a decision."

"How was the problem corrected?" Grandpa asked.

"After a couple of months of painful quota driven *Blitz* activity, one area manager requested and received permission to post a *Blitz* facilitator position. However, rather than recruit and hire a trained and experienced professional for the job, we promoted one of our untrained Quality Assurance Technicians into the position. All *Blitzing* responsibilities were quickly dumped onto the facilitator."

"Dare I ask? How did that turn out?" Grandpa questioned.

"Terrible. Things really unraveled during one particular *Blitz* event. One manager wanted to increase productivity in his area of the plant. He already had a solution in mind, but since there was a *Blitz* quota to meet, he solicited the *Blitz* facilitator to lead a cross-functional team to increase productivity. About halfway through the *Blitz* process, the area manager checked in with the *Blitz* team to see how they were progressing. When he found out that the team was going down a path he did not agree with, he handed the team his preconceived solution. The team members were furious, and walked out, refusing to continue their participation in the *Blitz*."

"I can't say that I blame them," Grandpa interjected.

"I don't either. But things went from bad to worse when the Union Leadership committee members learned what had taken place," Leon added.

"How so?" Grandpa asked.

"They became outspoken, and began posting propaganda on the plant bulletin boards. Union members were advised not to participate on *Blitz* teams. Union leaders said that *Blitzes* were the company's way of tricking employees into accepting their ideas, and that *Lean Manufacturing* was going to cause job losses in the long run."

"How did the union employees respond to their leader's campaign?" Grandpa asked.

"They took their suggestions to heart. It was nearly impossible to get hourly employees to participate on *Blitz* teams."

Grandpa stopped Leon and said, "This is a lot for an old man to absorb. Let me see if I have understood you so far."

"Okay," Leon replied.

Grandpa began to summarize what he had heard, "HFS was suffering from decreased profitability and the investors directed Mr. Ritz to fix the problem. Mr. Ritz promptly threatened Mr. Gump to fix the problem, saying that if he didn't it would cost him his job. Mr. Gump, looking for a quick fix, chose *Lean Manufacturing* as his silver bullet. Even though he did not understand what *Lean Manufacturing* was, Gump retained Mr. Cuttmore, a business consultant, to assist with the *Lean* launch. Only a handful of managers and supervisors were invited to an overview presentation, excluding a large part of the leadership team."

"Don't forget that Mr. Gump had obtained approval from Mr. Ritz to move forward with the *Lean* implementation," Leon added.

"Oh yes, you mentioned that. It sounds like he wasn't very involved," Grandpa responded.

"No, he sure wasn't," Leon replied.

Grandpa continued, "Mr. Cuttmore recommended that HFS should get focused and develop a unique selling position to thwart competitive threats. Mr. Gump dismissed Cuttmore's suggestion with a know-it-all attitude. And to top it off, he berated a manager in front of his peers and reports when he questioned Gump's decision."

Leon interjected, "I don't know that Gump portrayed a know-it-all attitude, but he did dismiss the consultant's *Value Proposition* recommendation."

Grandpa replied, "You're right Leon, I added the attitude part myself."

Grandpa continued by saying, "The consultant helped manufacturing managers to see the waste in the manufacturing process by *Value Stream Mapping* the current state flow of products and information. They found that only 3 percent of the manufacturing lead-time added value."

Leon said, "That's correct."

"Gump said that Mr. Cuttmore's presentation directed HFS to use *Blitz* teams to eliminate waste from the business, and Gump ended the contract with the consultant and promptly assigned *Blitz* quotas to the manufacturing managers. Is that right?" Grandpa asked.

"I'm not sure who ended the contract, but the bottom line was we were on our own," Leon said.

Grandpa replied, "I see. However, you did say the managers were not trained in *Blitz* facilitation techniques, and some passed the responsibility onto their supervisors, who were not trained either."

"That's right," Leon replied.

Grandpa continued, "There was no formal announcement to the organization, explaining what was happening, or why, and that resulted in workplace confusion. Managers and supervisors lacked project management skills and as a result did a poor job planning *Blitzes*. Their poor planning resulted in frustrated team members and poor outcomes. In their haste to pass the buck, managers quickly created a new *Blitz* facilitator position that was filled by an internal candidate who also lacked project management skills. To top things off, so-called empowered cross-functional *Blitz* teams were only empowered to effect improvements, if the outcomes were in alignment with manager's preconceived outcomes. Because of all that transpired, the Union Leaders have launched a campaign against the support of *Lean Manufacturing*. Have I got it right?" Grandpa asked.

Leon, who sat speechless, could only nod his head in agreement.

Shaking his head in disbelief, Grandpa added, "If I had to guess, I would bet my paycheck that management blames the union for the *Blitz* failures."

The look on Leon's face revealed that Grandpa was dead on with his assumption.

Pseudo Executive Officer

It was nearing mid-day and both Leon and his grandpa were experiencing hunger pangs.

"Break open that lunch bag, and let's see what your grandma made for lunch," Grandpa instructed Leon, as he pointed his finger towards the brown grocery bag tucked away in the front of the boat.

Leon smiled and anxiously replied, "Sure thing!"

Leon reached forward, grabbed the bag, and opened it with hungry anticipation. "Looks like chicken breast sandwiches with lettuce, tomato, and mayo, on whole wheat bread," Leon said with satisfaction.

"Great! Take one for yourself, and pass me one," Grandpa told Leon.

Leon eagerly complied with his Grandpa's request.

After they had patted down the appetites, quenched their thirst, and reminded each other to thank Grandma for the fine lunch when they got home, Leon picked up the story where he had left off.

"Mr. Gump had put all of his eggs in one basket when he told Mr. Ritz that *Lean Manufacturing* was going to solve their problems. With all of the pushback that was coming from supervisors, managers, and union members, Gump knew that a change would be necessary, and that's where I come in," Leon told his Grandpa.

"We were about one year into our failing *Lean* transformation efforts when Mr. Gump called me into his office. He told me what a great asset I was to the organization, and how impressed he was with my performance as a supervisor. He said he was impressed with my ability to win friends and resolve conflicts. After he was done buttering me up, Gump told me that the current *Blitz* facilitator wasn't working out, and he needed someone new to focus on the *Lean Enterprise* transformation. He asked if I would be willing to take on the responsibility. He said it would be a promotion and that I would report directly to him in a key support role, but that the area managers would still report directly to him."

"Please tell me you didn't accept his offer?" Grandpa painfully asked.

"I knew that the transformation was floundering, but I was intrigued by *Lean* and saw it as the way of the future. I accepted his offer. Before I left his office, Gump told me that we needed to keep *Blitzing*, just like Mr. Cuttmore's presentation had recommended."

Grandpa interrupted, "I thought you said that it was difficult to get employees to participate in *Blitzes*."

"I did. Nevertheless, I didn't want to disappoint Mr. Gump. I began encouraging managers to let me facilitate *Blitzes* in their areas. The responses to my requests were less than enthusiastic. Managers told me to go ahead and *Blitz* if I wanted, but that they were too busy to participate themselves. Several told me straight out that they were tired of fighting with the Union. I wondered if they were really tired of fighting with the Union, or if that was only an excuse."

"What do you mean, Leon?" Grandpa asked.

Leon replied, "In hindsight, I think some managers resented the fact that Gump had assigned a peer to lead improvements in their areas. I suspected that some of the managers opposed *Blitzes* because they enjoyed the recognition they received for being good *firefighters,* and the thought of relinquishing their authority to an empowered cross-functional team may have been unsettling to them."

"Couldn't there have been another possibility?" Grandpa asked.

"Like what?" Leon replied.

"Well, don't take this the wrong way Leon, but you said that the only training you received in Lean was a 180-slide PowerPoint presentation delivered by Mr. Cuttmore a year earlier. Don't you think the managers could have questioned your skills and abilities?"

"Maybe at first, but I worked hard to get up to speed on *Lean Manufacturing.* I read every book I could find on the subject, attended several different training seminars, and completed a Lean Certificate program at the local Technical College. Although I was not an expert on the subject, I had developed a working knowledge of *Lean* and felt comfortable educating others and facilitating *Blitzes*," Leon replied to his grandpa.

"I'm proud of you Leon. You recognized your weakness and took decisive action to correct it. You told me how the managers responded to your promotion, but I'm curious how the hourly employees responded."

"Most were supportive and I received a lot of congratulations. However, there were still some cynics in the plant. For example, shortly after the announcement was made that I had accepted the *Lean Manufacturing* Manager's role, I was walking through the factory when an employee approached me and asked when they could do a *Blitz* in their area. I was very excited that someone was already requesting a *Blitz*. I asked them what process in their area needed improvement. To which they replied sarcastically, 'Oh nothing, I was just wondering when we would be able to throw work over the wall to someone else, just like the last *Blitz* team did to us.' I suspected that HFS's *Lean Enterprise* transformation was going to be an uphill journey."

"What did you do next?" Grandpa asked.

"I wanted a better understanding of our current situation, so I met with those people that had been most involved with the *Lean* transformation initiative to date. I asked them to summarize HFS's *Lean* implementation plan. Everyone looked at me as though I was speaking a foreign language. Then I asked them how they were measuring our transformational progress. They said the only thing they were tracking were the number of *Blitz* events conducted. I walked to the easel, picked up a magic marker and drew a vertical line down the center of the flipchart paper. I wrote WELL DONE at the top of the left column, and OPPOR-TUNITIES FOR IMPROVEMENT at the top of the right. I told the group that I wanted to learn from their efforts, and asked them to help me fill in the blanks under both headings relative to the *Lean* transformation efforts. After about thirty minutes of brainstorming, the left column had one entry: Tracking *Blitz* events. The right column had run over onto several sheets."

"Good for you Leon! Smart leaders recognize that if they do not understand the past, they will likely repeat mistakes that others have made before them. I should know, I taught history for 38 years," Grandpa said. "What did you do with the information you collected?" Grandpa asked.

"I thanked everyone for their time and input, and concluded the fact-finding meeting. I retreated to my office and scoured over the list. I also reviewed previous *Blitz* team's meeting notes, *Value Stream Maps*, training presentations, and any other *Lean Enterprise* meeting notes I could get my hands on. After careful review of all the materials and information I gathered, it had become apparent that we were on a journey that had no course or destination," Leon explained to his grandpa.

"I don't enjoy telling you this Leon, but it sounds to me like Gump had you set up for failure," Grandpa said with a compassionate tone.

"Blinded by my eagerness to climb the corporate ladder, I didn't see that at the time, but now that I look back on it, I think you're right," Leon responded.

"However, I wasn't about to give up. The Military taught me many things during my tour; failure is not an option, being one of them."

"So what did you do?" Grandpa asked.

"I called Mr. Cuttmore and explained what was going on. He told me he was not surprised. Stunned, I asked him to explain. He told me that he had cautioned Gump about launching a Lean journey prematurely. He told me that he had reminded Gump of his concerns after we had created the *Value Stream Maps*, and that is when Gump thanked him for his services and said that we would handle it from here."

"Sounds to me like Gump wanted to save a little time and money, so he shortcut the process," Grandpa said.

"I didn't know what to think. I wanted to give Mr. Gump the benefit of the doubt, so I contacted several additional *Lean* consultants and explained our situation. They all told me that many organizations experience similar problems, and that unless we took immediate corrective action, we were going to suffer a similar fate, DOING *LEAN* rather than BECOMING *LEAN*."

"What type of corrective action did they recommend?" Grandpa asked.

"They suggested that HFS retain the services of someone who had extensive practical application experience in leading a successful *Lean* transformation. They referred to this person as a *Sensei* (teacher)," Leon replied.

"How did you respond to their suggestion?" Grandpa asked.

"I agreed with them. Even though I had developed a good working knowledge of *Lean*, I lacked practical application experience. I believed that we would benefit from the experience of someone that had been there, done that. We needed a *Lean Sensei* to guide us on our journey."

"Your father should be very proud of you Leon. It takes a mature person to admit they don't have all the answers. So what did you do with the consultants' advice?" Grandpa asked.

"I met with Mr. Gump and asked if we could retain the services of a *Lean Sensei* to shorten our learning curve. His voice said he would be willing to review any proposals that I obtained, but his body language told me something different."

"But I didn't give Gump the chance to change his mind. I quickly obtained proposals from three different firms, and presented them to Mr. Gump."

"How did he respond?" Grandpa asked.

"He ranted and raved, saying there was no way the business could afford to pay what the consultants were asking. I left Gump's office feeling pretty deflated."

"How were you able to bounce back?" Grandpa asked.

"I knew that there was value in learning from others, and I wasn't about to give up. I contacted some of the references that the consultants had provided me with their proposals. I found that most were very open about sharing their *Lean* transformation experiences. Through my efforts, I was developing an informal *Lean Manufacturers* Association," Leon told his Grandpa.

Just then, Grandpa's rod tip bent sharply, nearly curving the rod in two. Grandpa gripped the handle as tightly as he could and reefed back on the rod to set the hook. He could feel the extreme weight of what was on the other end of his line. Suddenly, his rod tip snapped upwards and the line went slack causing Grandpa to tip over backwards, nearly falling out of the boat. Grandpa, shaken but unhurt, sat back up and slowly reeled his line in to find that his jig was gone.

Grandpa, being hard on himself, said, "That was a big fish, and I blew it."

Leon, hearing the disappointment in his grandpa's voice, tried to console him, "Don't be so hard on yourself. For all we know, it could have been a big snapping turtle. Here, hand me your line and I'll tie you on a new jig."

Plotting Our Course

While Leon re-rigged Grandpa's fishing line, Grandpa asked Leon, "What did you learn from the people you spoke with about their *Lean* implementation efforts?"

Leon replied, "They all provided a lot of good advice, but there were a few common themes that I heard from nearly every one of them.

1. Senior Management must understand, lead, and be actively involved in the Lean Transformation process

2. Adopt a 'no employment loss' policy to encourage everyone's participation

3. Gather the VOICE OF OUR CUSTOMERS before attempting to create flow."

"Sounds like good advice. Did they recommend anything else?" Grandpa asked.

"Yes. They all recommended the use of a *Sensei*, but I knew that was out of the question," Leon replied.

Grandpa said, "From what you have told me, it sounds like HFS was on a path that was very different from those that you spoke with. So what did you do to correct it?"

"I developed a summary of my findings and scheduled a meeting with Mr. Gump," Leon said.

Grandpa asked, "Weren't you nervous?"

"Absolutely, I had no idea how he would react to what I was about to say. Nevertheless, I knew that continuing down the path we were currently on was leading nowhere fast. It needed to be done, and it was my responsibility," Leon replied.

"I'm very proud of you Leon. Not many people would be willing to take a risk like that," Grandpa said, as he placed his hand on Leon's shoulder.

Leon thanked his grandpa for the compliment and continued sharing his story.

"When I met with Gump, I explained what I had found, and recommended that we suspend all *Blitz* activity and focus on creating a *Lean* transformation plan. I didn't bother to bring up the *Sensei* topic. To my disbelief, and relief, Gump agreed with my recommendation. But he told me that time was of the essence, and I only had one month to develop the plan."

"Was that enough time to develop the plan?" Grandpa asked.

Leon replied, "It had to be, that's all the time I was allotted. I didn't waste any time. Over the next month, I involved members of the Union Leadership Committee and Management to assist me in the development of a *Lean* transformation plan."

"We didn't have time to develop a full-blown *Value Proposition*, but it was too important to ignore altogether. I involved our Sales and Marketing staff, and they worked with our customers to gain a better understanding of what they valued."

"Armed with our customers' values, we created a common vision in which we would be working towards. We had our destination, but we needed to know our starting point. When we took a closer look at our *Current State Value Stream Maps*, we found that we had only mapped the common product flows and excluded all of the products that were really disrupting our production. We needed to define our various product flow families and make new maps, fast!"

"After we defined our product flow families, and created new *Current State Value Stream Maps*, they depicted a very different image than the first maps. Product flows and waste were much more obvious to everyone who viewed the maps."

"We also looked at the organization from a Human Resource perspective. We concluded that HFS leaders lacked the necessary knowledge and skill-sets to lead, support, and more importantly, sustain a *Lean Enterprise* transformation."

Grandpa asked, "What type of knowledge and skill-sets did they need to have?"

"They needed to have a thorough understanding of *Lean Manufacturing* principles, and they needed to know how and when to use the various process improvement tools within the *Lean* tool chest. But, in order to capitalize their knowledge, they would need to develop respectful and trusting relationships with their reports," Leon replied.

Although Grandpa already knew the answer, he asked Leon anyway just to see what he thought. "Why is the respect and trust so important?"

Leon got very passionate as he responded. "It's vital to have employees involved in the continuous improvement of their work process! No one knows the intricacies of a job better than the person completing the work. If employees are involved in developing the new process, they have *ownership* in it. If they are not involved, it belongs to someone else. The likelihood of sustaining improvements without ownership is extremely low, unless the process is physically altered so that it cannot be done another way. I have found that most people resist *being* changed. In fact, the only group of people that I have found that likes *being* changed, are wet babies."

Grandpa laughed hysterically at Leon's pun. As he regained his composure, Grandpa pulled out a red-checkered handkerchief from his shirt pocket and wiped tears of laughter away from his eyes, and said, "Wet babies like being changed. I have to remember that one. Please, go on."

Leon continued, "However, without mutual trust and respect it is very hard to get people involved. We found that out the hard way during our first year of *Blitzing*."

Grandpa clenched his hand into a fist, pointed his index finger towards the sky and shouted, "BINGO! I don't think that I am the exception when I say, if I don't trust or respect someone, it's highly unlikely that I am going to follow their lead."

Leon, satisfied that he had answered his grandpa's question, continued explaining how the *Lean* implementation plan was developed. "Once we had a clear picture of our starting point and knew our destination, deciding how we were going to get there was fairly easy. Our implementation plan consisted of three phases:

> A. Develop a foundation and infrastructure that would support our *Lean Enterprise* transformation

B. Pilot *Lean Manufacturing* in a small area of the plant

C. Launch our *Lean Enterprise* transformation journey

"Without going into too much detail, would you please briefly explain each of the phases for me, Leon?" Grandpa requested.

"If I get too deep, just stop me."

Leon touched on the high points explaining, "Phase one focused on building trust and relationships, and included actions such as: development of an employee redeployment plan that allowed for business expansion rather than layoffs; leadership training and development; relationship building; an all employee performance based reward system; and lots of open, honest, two-way communication. Phase two would move us into the practical application of *Lean Manufacturing* in a small controlled environment. This would allow us to learn from our mistakes and minimize any collateral damage. It was also part of our product family realignment. High-touch, labor intensive, products would be taken out of the mainstream production and set up in a *Lean Manufacturing* work cell.

This would increase the velocity of our products throughout all production areas. Phase three was the launch of our *Lean Enterprise* initiative. We were going to continue with manufacturing improvements, and expand waste reduction efforts into the administrative areas of our business and even outside of our business to our suppliers and customers."

"WOW! That sounds like an awful lot of work," Grandpa exclaimed. "So what did you do with your implementation plan?" He asked.

"We compiled our plan into a report and presented it, along with the new *Current and Future State Value Stream Maps*, to Mr. Gump."

"How did he react to your proposal?" Grandpa asked.

"He seemed somewhat receptive to the idea, but was not willing to make a commitment at the time. He said he would get back to me in a couple of weeks. The wait was a period of high anxiety, but Mr. Gump finally called me into his office. When I went in, I could tell he was in a good mood. He immediately congratulated

70

me on the fine work, and said that Mr. Ritz and the Board Members loved the implementation plan. I was very proud, but knew that many minds worked collaboratively to develop the plan, and I could not accept the credit myself. I told Mr. Gump that I didn't develop the plan by myself, and that many people had a hand in its development."

"Give credit where credit's due. I always say," Grandpa interjected.

"Absolutely. Can you believe that Gump did not make the time to thank them personally? He asked me to pass on his thanks for him," Leon said, with a look of disgust on his face.

"I can't say that I would be surprised, based upon everything you have told me so far," Grandpa responded.

"I must confess, in spite of Gump's unwillingness to thank others directly, I was on cloud nine. I was confident that we were going to satisfy our customers' needs, grow the business by crushing our competition, and secure HFS employee's futures for many years to come."

Sharing Leon's excitement, Grandpa said, "Well...tell me what happened next!"

A Shortcut to *Lean*?

"You won't believe it," Leon told his Grandpa.

"What? Tell me, what happened?" Grandpa asked, with anticipation.

Leon replied, "Gump dropped a bomb. Not just a little hand grenade either, but a 100-megaton nuclear warhead. He told me that he had chosen an area to pilot the *Lean* implementation, and work would begin in two weeks. I could not believe what I was hearing. We were going to completely skip the phase one activities and go straight to phase two!"

"Why on Earth would he do that?" Grandpa asked.

"I'm not sure. Nevertheless, I felt sick to my stomach when he told me. It was probably a side effect of the radioactive fallout," Leon replied with levity.

Always appreciative of a good joke, Grandpa laughingly said, "You sure have a way with words, Leon."

Leon gave his grandpa a moment to collect his composure and then continued.

"I asked Gump about the phase one action items, and he said that those would come naturally though our transformation efforts."

"How did you respond to that statement?" Grandpa asked.

Leon replied, "I stared back at him in disbelief for a moment. Then I politely reminded him of the union's concern about employment loss associated with waste reduction activities, and asked if it was going to be addressed."

Grandpa eagerly asked, "So, how did he respond?"

Leon took a deep long breath and said, "Mr. Gump took on a very serious expression, and told me, 'Look, I'm going to be totally honest with you. I know you would like me to address the organization and commit to them that their employment is not at risk because of our *Lean Enterprise* transformation. The unfortunate reality is our manufacturing costs are too high and concessions need to be made. People *are* going to lose their jobs because of the improvements that we make, PERIOD!'"

"How were you supposed to get people involved in change, when they knew the very improvements they were helping to make could cost them their jobs?" Grandpa asked.

Leon responded, "I asked Gump that very question, and he told me to just do my best."

Leon's Grandpa wanted to speak, but he just sat speechless with his lower jaw hanging slightly open. His brain was not capable of processing that kind of logic. His thoughts became congested and jammed-up like rush hour traffic in New York City.

Leon continued, "I left Gump's office feeling like I had been used. Perhaps I was too naïve, or maybe I had been too much of an optimist, but I viewed *Lean* as a business growth process, and it was apparent that Gump was going to use it as a tool to cut direct labor to make himself look good in the eyes of Mr. Ritz, the Board of Directors, and the owners. My intuition told me that things were going to get worse rather than better."

The breeze had died down and the weather was heating up. It had been more than 3-hours since either Leon or his grandpa had a fish bite, but the same could not be said about mosquito bites. Leon, hoping to escape the swarm of mosquitoes that buzzed around his head, and suspecting that the fish had moved into deeper water to escape the mid-day heat, swatted a mosquito and asked his grandpa, "Do you think the fish moved into deeper water?"

"Could be. Go on with the rest of your story while I row us out to deeper water. If we get real lucky, there might be a breeze out there to blow these gosh darn mosquitoes away!" Grandpa howled as a mosquito plunged its' steely stinger into the back of his neck.

Grandpa grabbed hold of the oars and quickly rowed the boat away from the shallows that surrounded the boat docks, and headed out towards the deepest part of the Lake.

Damn the Torpedoes, Full Speed Ahead

"So what happened next?" Grandpa asked while he rowed.

"Gump met with the Union Leadership team and told them of his plans to implement *Lean* in a pilot area at HFS. He also told them that by his estimates, the improvements would reduce the need for direct labor employees by about a dozen. The Union Leaders told him that they would not support the initiative. But when Gump threatened to move the work and jobs to a Right-to-Work State, they had a quick change of heart."

"Sounds like Gump was playing hard-ball," Grandpa said.

Leon replied, "Oh he was dead serious. There was no doubt in my mind that Gump would have moved all operations if the Union leaders had not conceded. However, his strong-arm approach did nothing to help build a collaborative work environment."

"I'll bet. What happened next?" Grandpa asked with a morbid sense of curiosity.

"Gump hand-picked Thomas Duff to manage the new pilot area. Duff had 15 years of manufacturing experience, but he had only been at HFS a little over two years. Duff didn't know the first thing about *Lean Manufacturing*, but Gump really didn't care about that. He knew that Duff had a knack for meeting production demands, and that was good enough for him."

"Sounds like Duff was a micro-manager with a *my-way or the highway* leadership style. How did that affect the pilot area?" Grandpa asked.

Leon replied, "Since all of the foundational work outlined in phase one of the *Lean* implementation plan had been ignored, there was a ton of work to be done, way more than Duff had signed up for."

"The new game plan was to educate pilot area employees in *Lean Manufacturing*, and provide *just-in-time* training to facilitate the transformation."

"Shortly after I supplied the pilot area employees with a *Lean Manufacturing* overview, I kicked-off a 5S event to get the workplace clean and organized, and to re-instill manufacturing discipline into the workforce."

"What is 5S?" Grandpa asked.

"It's short for: Sort, Set-in-order, Shine, Standardize, and Sustain. The 5S process focuses on productivity gains through housekeeping, organization, and instilling discipline into the workforce," Leon replied.

"How did that turn out?" Grandpa asked.

Leon replied with disgust, "Not well. Duff chose not to participate in the training. He was only concerned with production, and he refused to provide employees the time they needed to get their work areas clean and organized. He kept creating excuses saying that production needed to come first. The area actually got more dirty and disorganized over the next couple of months."

"How did Gump respond?" Grandpa asked.

"He was disappointed. But he was under a lot of pressure from Mr. Ritz to fix the entire business, so he decided we needed to jump right into phase three rather than correct the issues in the pilot area."

"You have got to be kidding," Grandpa said with disbelief.

Leon replied, "I wish I was. Gump shocked everyone at the next monthly management meeting when he announced that we needed to complete the following objectives over the next twelve months:

- Implement 5S throughout the entire facility

- Conduct a minimum of two Blitz events every month

- Transform our manufacturing processes to reflect our *Future State Value Stream Maps*"

"Gump made it clear that all of the activities were expected to be done in addition to everyone's daily functional responsibilities, and that all salaried employees would support the *Lean* transformation or they would find themselves looking for a new job."

"We 5S'd administrative offices and kicked-off two *Blitzes* every month. We had some good success with workplace organization in most of the offices. *Blitzes* however, were a different story. Managers really did not care how the *Blitzes* turned out; they just needed to get the box checked to keep Gump off their backs."

"The lack of collaboration and basic manufacturing disciplines made the *Future State Value Stream* transformation efforts slow and painful."

"What do you mean by manufacturing disciplines?" Grandpa asked.

"There are five basic areas of manufacturing that need to be managed: Machines, Materials, Manpower, Methods, and Measurements. They are called the 5M's for short. We did a poor job of managing them in the past, and as a result, there was a lot that needed fixing. That really compounded everyone's workload, overtaxing our limited resources. Emotions ran high and tempers grew short."

"To make matters worse, several months into our efforts the market took a significant downturn. The profit and loss statement reflected the slump in sales. Gump reacted, saying that a lay-off was necessary. He instructed the Human Resource manager to lay off 20 percent of the hourly employees, and 10 percent of the salaried group. Employees associated the layoff with all of the *Lean* activities that had taken place. Gump tried to explain that the layoff was due to unforeseen market conditions, but employees did not trust him, and they were not buying his story."

"Did you put the Lean transformation on hold after the layoff?" Grandpa asked.

"No. The *5S*, *Blitz*, and *Future State* objectives remained in effect. Employees who survived the reduction-in-force found themselves spread a mile wide and an inch deep. Nothing was being done well. Marketable employees, with good skills, began seeking other employment opportunities. Some were hired by HFS's competitors. A lot more would surely have left, if they didn't have such strong ties to Windy Point."

Grandpa interjected, "Surely the resignation of good employees captured someone's attention."

Leon replied, "Oh yes. Mr. Gump recognized that he needed to stop the bleeding that the organization was experiencing. He held a meeting with all of the employees and told everyone that the layoffs were behind them, and that no one's employment was in jeopardy because of their future involvement in *Lean* activities. He encouraged everyone to participate in the *Lean* transformation."

"How did people respond to what Gump had to say?" Grandpa asked.

Leon replied, "The reactions were mixed. Most of the salaried employees I spoke with believed Gump, and were willing to get involved. However, the Union Leaders took a different position. I met with them two days after the meeting and asked if they would actively support the *Lean* implementation effort. They said that they recognized the value that *Lean Manufacturing* could bring, but flat out told me they did **not** trust Gump. They suspected that Gump was going to use *Lean* to cut more jobs, and that they would rather see HFS go under than to be misled by Gump again."

"Whoa. Did I hear you correctly? The Union Leadership team told you that they would rather see the doors close than to be lied to again?" Grandpa asked Leon.

"Yes, you heard me right," Leon replied.

"What did you do with that information?" Grandpa asked.

"I knew that Gump needed to know how the Union Leaders felt. So I scheduled a meeting with Gump and told him what they said."

"How did Gump react to that slap in the face?" Grandpa asked.

"He got very upset, and called the Union Leaders a bunch of blockheads, saying they would look a gift horse in the mouth if given the chance. He told me how he receives letters every day from Right-to-Work States, offering tax and utility breaks for businesses that relocate to their states. He assured me that if the Union continued to push back, he would unbolt all of the equipment, and move operations to a Right-to-Work State."

Grandpa asked, "How did you respond to Gump's reaction towards the Union Leader's comments?"

"I told Gump that I wasn't sure how I should proceed with the *Lean* implementation, given the Union Leader's position. Gump told me that he had grown tired of dealing with the Union and that we needed to take a different approach," Leon replied.

"What did he mean by that?" Grandpa asked.

"Gump told me that we were not going to seek the union's involvement and participation any longer. He said they had their chance and they blew it! Gump said we needed to move forward with the achievement of the *Future State*, with or without the Union's support. I was torn by Gump's comments," Leon said.

"How so?" Grandpa asked.

"I believe that *Lean Enterprise* transformations are best achieved through the collaborative efforts of everyone, and that a 'ram it down their throats' approach had a high likelihood of failure. However, I was upset with the Union Leaders for not supporting the transformation. They were asked to participate, and they chose not to for stated reasons. I could see both positions, and felt stuck in the middle."

"So what did you do?" Grandpa asked.

"After that meeting, I went to my office, shut the door, and thought long and hard about resigning. After I calmed down, I decided to keep my job and resume work on the *Future State* to the best of my abilities, as Gump had instructed me."

Grandpa didn't respond at first. He just stared quietly into the water as he jigged his bait ever so slowly. After a few moments, Grandpa said, "Please go on."

Leon continued, "Over the course of the next several months, we streamlined our manufacturing processes by: realigning product families, installing some new equipment, reducing batch sizes, improving mechanical reliability, defining and implementing quality standards, implementing material replenishment pull and flow systems, creating standard work, and 5Sing. Our efforts resulted in nearly a 40 percent reduction of work-in-process inventories, and we cut our manufacturing cycle time by 70 percent for several product families."

Grandpa looked up from the water and said, "That's great! So why the long face?"

"Well, as soon as the improvements were in place, Gump eliminated a bunch of hourly positions, and we had more layoffs. Employees do not feel secure at HFS, and many have sought alternative employment. It seems like every week someone else quits. Morale hit a new low, and work is not fun any more. The atmosphere feels like that of a morgue, and employees that I once had a good relationships with no longer speak to me," Leon replied.

Grandpa interrupted, "Wait a minute. I thought you told me that Gump promised no more employment loss."

"I did. However, Gump justified his actions because of the position the Union Leaders had taken," Leon replied.

"You have gotten yourself into a tough spot Leon," Grandpa said in an empathetic tone.

"Tell me about it," Leon replied with a heavy sigh.

Calling on Allies

Grandpa stopped rowing and asked Leon to drop the anchor. "There is a nice drop-off that runs parallel to the boat right over there," Grandpa said to Leon as he pointed towards the direction of the drop-off.

Leon hastily dropped the anchor over the edge of the boat, and in the process got a taste of Stainy Lake as water splashed up into his face.

"How does the lake taste?" Grandpa asked, doing his best to hold back his urge to laugh.

"Like a raw fish salad, with a hint of algae," Leon replied.

After the boat was anchored, both men cast their rods towards the drop-off and began jigging their bait along its edge. Their suspicions quickly paid off. On his first cast, Grandpa felt a familiar tap on his rod from a fish that had inhaled his bait. Grandpa set the hook, and after a short fight, he hoisted the walleye into the boat without the use of the net.

"Not as big as yours, but it's legal. Here, put it on the stringer," Grandpa boyishly giggled, as he handed Leon the fish.

Leon set his rod down and attempted to hook Grandpa's fish on the stringer. Out of the corner of his eye, he saw his own fishing rod's tip begin to twitch ever so slightly. Leon quickly dropped the stringer and Grandpa's fish into the bottom of the boat, grabbed his fishing pole, and jerked to set the hook.

"Did you get him?" Grandpa yelled.

"He's on, but it doesn't feel very big," Leon replied.

The little walleye didn't put up much resistance as Leon quickly reeled it in.

"Go back and send your grandpa," Leon said as he let the fish slide through his fingers back into the lake.

Leon sat his rod down and finished putting his grandpa's fish on the stringer. Both men re-tipped their jigs with fresh night crawlers and resumed fishing. Neither spoke much for the next five minutes or so.

Their total attention was focused on catching more fish.

Unfortunately, the action stopped just as quickly as it had started, and after a couple more minutes, Grandpa asked, "So what happened after the layoffs?"

"Well, about a month ago I was reflecting upon how we were going about our *Lean* implementation, and the seemingly negative impact it was having on everyone."

"I thought about all the books that I read describing *Lean Manufacturing*. They all made it seem so simple. I wondered what we were doing that was making it so difficult. As fate would have it, that same day, I received an invitation to a *Lean Manufacturing* conference. I thought the conference would provide an opportunity to learn what we were doing wrong, so I enrolled, and attended the conference a couple of weeks ago."

"What did you learn?" Grandpa inquired.

"While I was at the conference, I spoke with hundreds of people whose businesses were also on *Lean* journeys. I asked them to describe their *Lean* journey for me. I was surprised, and a little relieved, to hear only about 10 percent describe their journey as going well. Nearly 90 percent described their journeys as floundering or totally off track."

"Did you ask why?" Grandpa questioned.

"Yes. Most people were forthcoming with valuable information. I noticed common themes as my interviews progressed," Leon replied.

"Like what?" Grandpa asked.

Leon replied, "The 10 percent or so that described their implementation as going well commonly stated the following:"

1. The top leader in the organization is the *Lean Champion*, and even though they use a *Sensei* to keep themselves on track, the transformation is being driven by the *Champion*

2. Leaders are educated and understand *Lean Manufacturing* principles and tools; and they recognize

that *Lean* is a means to an end, and not an end in itself

3. They understand what their customers' value, and focus on delivering that value

4. The critical few business objectives are defined and closely monitored to foster success and avoid overload

5. All management members lead, support and are actively involved in the implementation process

6. There is a tenacious focus on results, and staying the course

7. Obstacles and anchor draggers are quickly removed

8. They have open, honest, frequent, two-way communication

9. There was a high degree of mutual trust throughout the organization; people feel valued, and are involved

10. They realize that their competition is outside of their own facility, and they strive to create

teamwork by creating a blame-free environment and focus on improving the process.

"The 90 percent that described their implementation as floundering, or off track, routinely stated the following:"

1. *Lean* was initiated as a corporate directive, or internally by the top or second level leader, then implementation responsibilities were quickly delegated (or abdicated) to members of mid to lower levels of management

2. There is little or no understanding of *Lean* within the organization

3. They could not define their customer's values

4. Managers' objectives are frequently changing, conflicting, numerous, or occasionally lacking all together

5. Managers say they support *Lean*, but have little or no involvement in the actual implementation

6. The focus appears to be on activity rather than results

7. Obstacles are ignored, or shuffled around, but hardly ever removed

8. Communication is limited and typically only one way, top-down

9. There is little or no mutual trust within the organization; employees do not feel valued, and are not willing to become involved

10. There is a lot of finger pointing and affixing of blame. Internal conflict is ongoing, and external competition is rarely if ever discussed.

"Sounds like you identified crucial variables that can affect the degree of success organizations will have with their *Lean* implementation efforts," Grandpa said.

"I think I discovered something far more precious and greater than that!" Leon exclaimed.

"What do you mean?" Grandpa asked.

"I mean my findings are not confined to *Lean* transformational efforts. I believe you can substitute any business improvement initiative for the word *Lean* and the common themes would still apply. What I really discovered pertains to LEADER-SHIP!" Leon stated.

"I have to hand it to you Leon; I do believe you're right on the mark," Grandpa affirmed.

"I couldn't help but notice that you didn't mention Labor Unions in either list. Didn't they get mentioned during your interviews?" Grandpa asked.

"Good question. They did come up, but I decided not to include that feedback because most of the people that were present were from non-union businesses. However, when the topic did surface, people generally said their beef was with confining labor agreement language, and that they didn't have an issue with the concept of Labor Unions," Leon replied.

"Did they elaborate as to what types of language were so confining?" Grandpa asked.

"Yes. They gave examples of how prescriptive job descriptions and job assignment language has made it very difficult for them to make rapid improvements. For example, if one position was eliminated from an area, it could cause tens or hundreds of people to move jobs because of a bump-bid job assignment process. Leaders are hesitant to make the improvements needed in an area for fear of the disruptive ripple effects it could have," Leon replied.

"Where would you place Hardwood Floor Systems on the ten points you mentioned?" Grandpa asked.

"From my point-of-view, we are off track on all ten," Leon replied.

Price too High?

"You know what concerns me the most?" Leon asked.

"What's that?" Grandpa replied.

"I don't think that anyone will dispute the fact that we displayed poor leadership during our quest for waste elimination and cost reduction. We ignored the importance of people and relationships, and as a result, trust and respect is virtually non-existent. Employees do not feel valued, and many are seeking other employment opportunities. It's becoming increasingly difficult to attract good employees because of the negative reputation that HFS has earned."

"So what's your concern?" Grandpa asked.

"In spite of ourselves, we have managed to significantly reduce manufacturing cycle-times, slash work-in-process inventories, and improve productivity. However, I am concerned that these improvements have come at too high a price. If employees continue to leave, and we cannot attract good replacement workers, what will happen to the business in the long run?" Leon asked.

Before Grandpa could reply, Leon added, "I wish more business leaders truly understood and appreciated the competitive advantage *Lean Manufacturing* offers," Leon said.

Grandpa scoffed at Leon's statement, "Some competitive advantage. Sounds to me like HFS is at risk of going out of business."

Leon responded to his Grandpa's remarks by asking, "HFS was able to significantly reduce waste, while neglecting the importance of relationships, right?"

Grandpa nodded in agreement.

"Just imagine its full potential in an organization filled with mutual trust and respect, whose employees feel valued, and customer values are sought after and understood," Leon said.

For the first time Grandpa totally understood Leon's frustrations at work.

"Do you think I should leave HFS?" Leon asked, looking for guidance from his grandfather.

"I can't tell you what to do Leon. You must decide for yourself," Grandpa replied.

Leon quietly turned and stared down at the water.

Grandpa, sensing that Leon was struggling with the decision, offered the following thoughts. "History has proven, time, and time again, that unification plays a very important role in shaping our world. Successful leaders behave in a manner that promotes unification. They often start by defining a problem or opportunity, and then create goals that they believe will improve the situation. If other people need to be involved, the desired outcome must inspire them, or they will not be committed to its cause."

"This is where so many leaders get tripped up. Their motives are often selfish, seeking wealth and power only for themselves. Most people have good intuition, and usually see through the lies and deceptive tactics of those who seek to benefit only themselves at the expense of others."

"I have always believed that culture is a direct reflection of leadership no matter where you work. Think about the work culture that existed under John Rodman's leadership. Why was it so different from the culture that was created under Eastwood and HFS leaders?"

"From what you told me, it sounds like HFS employees believed that Gump's goals were to line his own pockets at the expense of others. I do not know of very many people who would sign up for that cause. Do you?" Grandpa asked Leon.

"No, I sure don't," Leon replied.

"John Rodman's father was correct when he said that hard work and perseverance alone will not guarantee success. Leaders must be trustworthy and respected in order to inspire others to follow them when the going gets tough."

"Do you think Mr. Gump has the trust and respect of the employees at Hardwood Floor Systems?" Grandpa asked.

Leon sat quietly, and thought about his Grandpa's question.

Where is the Captain?

Before Leon could respond to the question, Grandpa said, "I would like to summarize what I heard from you today with a short story."

Leon perked up and said, "I'm all ears."

Grandpa sat his fishing rod down, turned to look Leon squarely in the eye, and began to speak. "There once was a cruise ship named the HFS. It was a big old ship, and it had a leaky hull. One day Admiral Ritz ordered Captain Gump to fix the leaky HFS. Captain Gump heard of a port that was well known for its ability to repair crippled cruise ships. Its name was Port *Lean*. Captain Gump received permission from Admiral Ritz to take the HFS, its crew, and passengers to Port *Lean* for repairs."

"Gump told the crew and passengers they were going on a voyage, but he only told a few crewmembers they were heading to Port *Lean*."

"The crew conducted a pre-trip inspection of the vessel and found that it was not equipped with life rafts or personal flotation devices. The hull had a crack and the ship was taking on water. The bilge pump had shorted out years earlier, and had not been repaired. The crew informed Captain Gump of the problems they had found, and asked him what they should do."

"Captain Gump told the crew that all the repairs they needed would be found at Port *Lean,* and that they should cast off. The Captain informed the crew and passengers he would not be joining them on the voyage, but he would meet them at Port *Lean.* The Captain said he would be in contact via two-way radio if they needed anything."

"Shortly after the crew set out on their voyage, they realized that the Captain had not provided them with a navigational map, or safe travel coordinates. The crew was not sure how to get to Port *Lean* or how to avoid the hidden dangers that lurked just beneath the water's surface. The crew radioed the Captain and asked for directions."

"The Captain realized that he had not taken the time to get directions to *Lean*. However, he didn't want the crew to know that he didn't have directions either, and he surely wasn't about to contact the Coast Guard for assistance. If word got back to Admiral Ritz, Gump would surely lose his rank. Although the Captain did not know where Port *Lean* was, he knew he needed to provide direction quickly, or the crew would become suspicious. He told the crew to head up river against the current, and to keep going until they saw the beautiful port named *Lean*. The crew complied with the Captain's command."

"Due to its cracked hull, the ship was slowly filling with water, and the crew and passengers were getting nervous. The crew radioed the Captain and requested a new bilge pump. Captain Gump told the crew to increase their speed and let centrifugal force remove the water."

"The crew complied with the Captain's order. They increased speed and quickly ran into a submerged rock, widening the crack in the hull. The water began to flow in faster than ever. Passengers and crew grew increasingly concerned as the ship began to sink even faster."

"The crew radioed the Captain, and asked him what they should do. The Captain radioed back and said that the HFS needed saving at all costs. He ordered the crew to lighten the load by throwing passengers overboard. The crew complied with his command and began throwing passengers off the ship. This bought some time, but spread panic throughout the ship like a forest fire raging out of control. Passengers began locking themselves in their cabins, thinking that if they would not come out, they could not be thrown overboard. However, in their haste passengers forgot that the ship was sinking and if it went under they would drown in their locked cabins."

"The crew continued heading upstream, fighting the current in search of Port *Lean*. They had not gone much further when the ship struck a second rock, and the crack in the hull grew even wider. Water was pouring in, and the crew panicked. Crewmembers who knew how to swim jumped off the HFS and swam to the safety of passing ships. However, those who did not know how to swim, or were afraid of the swift current, were trapped on a sinking ship along with the passengers that remained locked in their cabins. The desperate crew radioed the Captain seeking help."

"Captain Gump responded, telling the crew to grab some buckets and bail the water out. The crew bailed as fast as they could. The passengers heard the commotion, and several ventured out of their cabins and pitched in. After the passengers had bailed themselves to exhaustion, the crew figured they were of no value and threw them overboard to lighten the load, as the Captain had ordered earlier."

"The crew managed to gain some additional time, but the ship was surely sinking as the water continued pouring in. The crew radioed the Captain and explained that they were in serious trouble, and requested permission to either alter their course, or to call the Coast Guard for rescue."

"The Captain thought about the crew's request. He was not sure what to do. If he authorized a delay, the Admiral would be very angry and possibly even revoke his commission. If he called in the Coast Guard, the Admiral would find out that he was not prepared for the voyage. If he ordered the crew to continue on, and the ship sank, the Admiral would have his head on a platter. The Captain was overwrought with a sinking feeling."

"He began to think about the old cliché, *The Captain always goes down with the ship*. In that moment, it dawned on him; he was not on the ship, he was on dry land. A sinister smile formed on Captain Gump's face as he radioed back to the crew."

"Where is crewman Leon? The Captain shouted into the microphone. 'He is standing right here, Captain,' the crew responded. The Captain said, 'Listen close, crewman Leon. You are the most experienced crewmember on board, and I have other more important matters that I need to tend to right now. I need you to take command of the HFS, however, remember that the crew still reports to me.' Captain Gump signed off the radio saying, 'Congratulations on your promotion Executive Officer Leon, and good luck!'"

"At that moment crewmen Leon knew he was in a no win situation. He realized he had become Captain Gump's sacrificial lamb."

After Grandpa finished his story, Leon sat quietly for a moment and then said, "You have a great way of putting things in perspective Grandpa."

"We had better call it a day. You know how your grandma worries if we are late," Grandpa said.

"Aye Aye, Captain," Leon replied as he snapped his grandpa a firm hand salute.

Grandpa returned the salute and said, "Not Captain Gump, I hope."

"Not in a million years!" Leon replied.

Grandpa grabbed hold of the oars and waited patiently as Leon hoisted and secured the anchor in the bow of the boat. After Leon was seated, Grandpa slowly rowed the boat back towards the public boat launch.

Leon stared across Stainy Lake at Gump's mansion and thought to himself. He realized he did not want to be a part of Captain Gump's *Titanic*-like voyage any longer. The thought of leaving Hardwood Floor Systems was unsettling at first, but Leon's fears quickly subsided as he felt a calling. Leon experienced an overwhelming desire to write about his experiences so that others would not have to endure the painful mistakes that plagued the leadership group at Hardwood Floor Systems during the attempted *Lean Transformation*. Leon knew his book would serve as a lighthouse equipped with a brilliant beacon to help guide lost and distressed passengers and crew reach their *Lean Enterprise* destinations safely!

Holding back tears of thankfulness, Leon looked at his Grandfather and said, "Thank you, from the bottom of my heart. How can I ever repay you?"

"You're welcome Leon. Spending the day with me fishing and involving me in your life is payment enough," Grandpa said with a smile.

The End.

Other Books from
Science & Humanities press

Other Books

Value Centered Leadership—A Survivor's Strategy for Personal and Professional Growth—Captain George A. Burk (2004) Principles of Leadership & Total Quality Management applied to all aspects of living. ISBN 1-888725-59-1, 5½X8¼, 120 pp, $16.95

50 Things You Didn't Learn in School–But Should Have: Little known facts that still affect our world today (2005) by John Naese. ISBN 1-888725-49-4, 5½X8¼, 200 pp, illustrated. $16.95

Youth Risk Behavior Surveillance Survey with Student Guide for Statistical Analysis in EXCEL, R. J. Banis, PhD & Centers for Disease Control Staff (2008) ISBN 1-888725-24-9, Heuristic Books, 8½X11, spiral bound, 250 pp, $28.95

Questionnaires--Practical Hints on How to Avoid Mistakes in Design and Interpretation-- By T.L.Brink, PhD, MBA (2004) Includes bibliographical references and index. ISBN 1-888725-74-5 6¼X8¼, 270pp, $18.95

Educators Discount Policy:

To encourage use of our books for education, educators can purchase three or more books (mixed titles) on our standard discount schedule for resellers. See

sciencehumanitiespress.com/educator/ educator.html for more detail or call

Science & Humanities Press,

PO Box 7151, Chesterfield MO 63006-7151

636-394-4950

Our books are guaranteed:

If a book has a defect, or doesn't hold up under normal use, or if you are unhappy in any way with one of our books, we are interested to know about it and will replace it and credit reasonable return shipping costs. Products with publisher defects (i.e., books with missing pages, etc.) may be returned at any time without authorization. However, we request that you describe the problem, to help us to continuously improve.

Books by Darrell Bender

Beyond Lean—Lessons for Leading Organizational Change, Darrell Bender (2006) ISBN 1-59630-016-7 A parable describing the promise and warning of the pitfalls in the transformations to a *lean manufacturing system* related from the diverse experience of Darrell Bender. 8½ X 5½ Paper, 112 pp. $16.95

Order Form

Item	Each	Quantity	Amount
Missouri (only) sales tax 6.075%			
Priority Shipping			$5.00
Total			

Name

Address

Heuristic Books
PO Box 7151
Chesterfield, MO 63006-7151
(636) 394-4950
Heuristicbooks.com
s.com

Heuristic Books

for Mathematics & Management Science
heuristicbooks.com

www.ingramcontent.com/pod-product-compliance
Lightning Source LLC
Chambersburg PA
CBHW071149200326
41519CB00018B/5161